DOMIN(

BEGINNERS:

How to Win Almost Every Game with Proven

Strategies & Secret Traps Used by Pros

Grant Dittman

3

Table of Contents

Introduction

Learning how to play dominoes is a necessary skill for every game enthusiast who enjoys socializing.

Don't worry if you've never played Dominoes before; this guide will walk you through the process. Dominoes is a game played by two or four people using twenty-eight oblong ivory pieces split by a black line in the middle and indented with spots, ranging from one to a double six.

The pieces are:

- double-blank
- ace-blank
- double-ace
- deuce-blank
- deuce-ace
- double-deuce
- trois-blank
- trois-ace
- trois-deuce
- double-trois
- four-blank

- four-ace
- four-deuce
- four-trois
- double-four
- five-blank
- five-ace
- five-deuce
- five-trois
- five-four
- double-five
- six-blank
- six-ace
- six-deuce
- six-trois
- six-four
- sixfive
- double-six.

Sometimes a double set is played with, of which double twelve is the highest.

There are numerous domino games that pass by various names but are quite comparable, and at times even indistinguishable, rules. Furthermore, there are numerous games that pass by similar name in different parts of the globe, however the rules varies from one part of the world to the other.

In numerous domino games, a line of tiles is formed on the table as players make their plays, normally, however not generally, by coordinating with the pips on the open finish of the domino. This development of tiles is known as the line of play. There are fundamental directions recorded here under Line of Play explicitly for those games.

As a result, I have put together this detailed explanation on how to play dominoes to get you up to speed. Let's get started.

Chapter 1: Introduction To Dominoes

Dominoes are an incredible game! It is a game that adults and children alike can enjoy, and it is a fantastic choice for a stay-at-home game night.

Dominoes are first mentioned in Song dynasty China, in the classic Former Events in Wulin (1232–1298). Dominoes were invented in Italy during the 18th century, although they are notably different from Chinese dominoes in a number of aspects, and there is no evidence that there is any connection between the two. European dominoes may have developed independently of one another, or they may have been introduced to Europe by Italian missionaries in China during the Renaissance period.

Domino Pieces

Dominoes are a type of game component that is small, flat, and rectangular in shape. Over the years, dominoes have been made from a variety of materials, including plastic, wood, bone, ivory, and stone. Individual domino pieces are commonly referred to as dominoes or tiles in a set.

Domino pieces are typically twice the length of their width and are precisely half the thickness of their width in order as to stand on edge without toppling over.

A domino can be any size, but the standard size is around one inch broad by two inches long.

A domino, like a playing card, has a front and a back. Each tile has a blank back or a design on it. A line runs down the middle of each tile's face, dividing it in half. In either half, numbers are represented by dots, generally referred to as pips, or by the absence of spots, which indicates zero.

When dominoes are manufactured, they have their pips uniformly molded or drilled and then painted. Domino sets are available in virtually every color combination. However, white dominoes with black pips and black dominoes with white pips are the most often used color combinations.

The number of pips on either half of a domino's face determines the name of the domino. For instance, the 3-5 dominoes is a domino face with three pips on one half and five pips on the other.

Doubles, or doublets, are dominoes with the same number of pips on either half of the face. A single domino, often known as a combination domino, has an odd number of pips on either half of the face.

A suit is made up of all tiles in a set that have the same number of pips on one end. Each double is associated with a single suit and singles are associated with 2 suits. For instance, the 3-5 can be classified as belonging to either the 3 or 5 suits.

Domino Set

A set of domino pieces is occasionally referred to as a deck.

The double-6, double-9, double-12, and double-15 sets are the four most popular domino sets. The majority of domino games are designed for use with a double-6 set. Numerous innovative and popular party games are designed to be played with larger sets (double-9, -12, and -15), which accommodate a greater number of players. However, the majority of game rules can simply be adjusted to accommodate a larger or smaller set of dominoes.

Each set of dominoes has all possible combinations of two numbers, ranging from zero (blank) to the set's maximum number of pips (for example, 12 in a double-12 set), as well as a double of each suit. Each pip combination appears exactly once in a set. A conventional double-6 domino set contains 28 tiles, seven of which are doubles and twenty-one of which are singles.

Each number occurs eight times in a double-6 set: once on each of the six tiles and twice on the double tile.

Now that you understand what dominoes are, it is time to learn the basic rules for dominoes.

Every player should thusly then play a tile onto the table situating it with the goal that it contacts one finish of the domino chain whose length subsequently slowly increases. A player may just play a tile which has upon it a number appearance toward one side of the domino chain or the other.

How the tiles are put gives a little piece of the diversion. Each tile being set should be situated so the two coordinating with closes are adjacent. Except if, the tile is a twofold, the tile can be put square in any of the three headings as long as the two coordinating with sides are contacting completely. Doubles are constantly positioned cross-ways across the finish of the chain. A tile played to a twofold (double) should likewise be set appropriately - opposite to the twofold contacting at its center. The state of the domino chain creates snake-line indiscriminately as indicated by the impulses of the players and the limitations that come with utilizing the playing surface.

In the event that a player can lay a domino, it should be played. In any case the player "knocks", or raps the table and play passes to the following player. The rival players will, obviously, give careful consideration of the numbers at present accessible on the table and attempt to guarantee that they are accessible in future too.....

How To Play Dominoes

There are numerous Dominoes varieties, and I will demonstrate how to play one of the most popular:

The Straight Dominoes Method.

Note

If there are four players, you can play in pairs with the person sitting opposite you, or you can individually play your own hand. If playing with more than four persons, utilize a double-12 set rather than a double-9 set.

A double-12 set includes 91 tiles, while a double-9 set includes 55 tiles

Step 1: Understanding the Tiles

The dots are referred to as pips, and each set contains 28 tiles.

Step 2: The Bonesyard

Lay out the tiles in such a way that the side with the dot of each tile is flat against the board surface. One player should shuffle the tiles thoroughly to determine who will play first.

Step 3: Determining Who Will Play First

To determining who will play first, allow each participant to draw one tile at random from the boneyard.

Begin by having everyone draw one tile, and whoever has the highest double will start first. If no double is drawn, the player that has the tile with the most pips (heaviest tile) will be the first.

Reintroduce the tiles to the pile and give them a brief shuffle. If you are tied on the draw, simply continue drawing until you are not.

Step 4: Getting Started

Each player should assemble a hand of seven dominoes. You may choose from any tile in the pile, but once a tile has been picked, it cannot be replaced. Arrange your seven dominoes in front of you such that they are visible to you, but keep them hidden from your opponent.

Step 5: Position Your First Tile in the Table Center

The player who drew the first tile may place whatever tile they like to begin the game. In such cases, placing a tile on which you are sure in your ability to construct for your next round is frequently a wise decision.

For instance, if you place a tile with 4 pips on one side and 3 on the other on the table or board, but do not have any other tiles with 4 or 3 pips on a side, you will be unable to play a turn until someone else places a tile with 4 or 3 pips on a side.

Step 6: Take Turns Using the Tiles in Your Hand to Construct Structures off the Tiles on the Board or Table.

Go round the board in an anti-clockwise fashion. Each turn, a player will place one tile on the board. That tile must have a side that corresponds to the open end of an existing domino on the table. Continue in this manner until someone exhausts all of their tiles.

When a tile with a blank side is laid down, you must use a tile that has the same blank side as the one you are laying down. For some other games, the blanks are left "wild," meaning they can be assigned any value. You may select any option that appeals to you!

Move 1

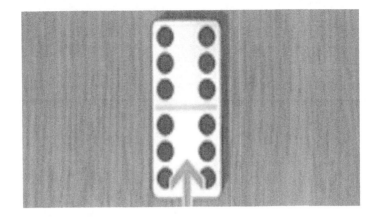

Move 2

17

Move 3

Move 4

Step 7

If You Are Unable to Play a Tile You Have, Simply Get Another Tile From the Boneyard or Draw Pile.

You can play a tile you picked from the draw pile if it corresponds to something on the board. Otherwise, place

the tile in your hand in addition to your previous tiles for
your opponent to take turn.

Move 1

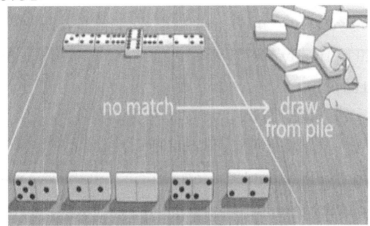

Move 2

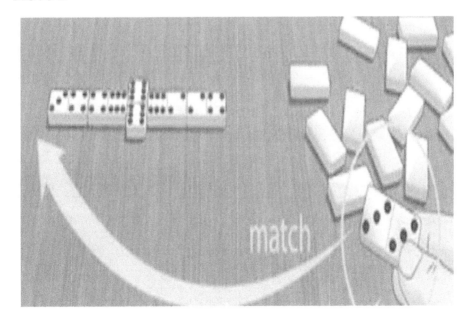

Step 8: To win a round, you must be the first to use up all of your dominoes (Placing all tiles on the board).

If you may have won the round on the board, this doesn't imply that you have the victory at this stage. Before the game will be finally over, you will have some more hands or round to play.

Note

Each round will have at least seven turns, but if everyone ends up picking up additional tiles from the draw pile, the game might run much longer.

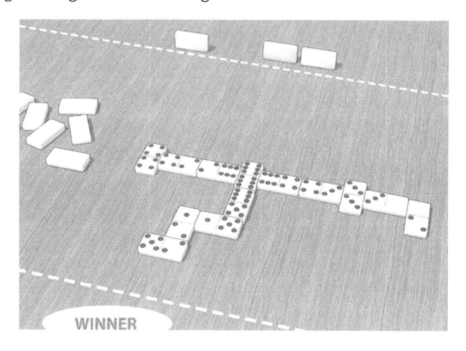

WINNER

Step 9: Count How Many Pips Are Left on the Tiles in Front of Each Player's.

Make a note add of the values in the winning player's column. The game is won by the person who reaches 100 points the quickest.

Because you must reach 100 points before the game ends, each player has several chances to win rounds and ultimately emerge victorious!

As you can see, dominoes are a game that is both entertaining and simple to understand.

As seen, with this straight domino method, you can now advance to learn other methods!

Chapter 2: Understanding Mexican Train Dominoes

In the game Mexican Train, each time a player places a domino on the table, that domino must adhere to the rules of standard domino play. This means that one end of the domino must touch the end of another domino that is already on the table, and the other end of the new domino must match (have the same number of dots as) the end of the domino that it is adjacent to.

The form of the domino chain, which is a snake-line, develops in a way that is completely random and is determined by the whims of the players as well as the constraints of the playing surface.

Each time a player puts a domino on the table in Mexican Train, it must adjusts to regular domino play. for example The domino should be put so one end is contacting the finish of a domino effectively on the table and to such an extent that the finish of the new domino matches (shows similar number of dabs or dots) the finish of domino it is adjacent to it. Except if the tile is a double, the tile can be set square in any of the three headings as long as the two coordinating with sides are contacting completely.

A domino having same number at both ends is known as a 'Double'. A Double as well, must be set neighboring a coordinating with end of a domino effectively on the table. Notwithstanding, doubles are constantly positioned oppositely across the finish of the domino that is now on the table to make a 'T'. A tile played to a double should likewise be set appropriately - perpendicular to the double contacting at its center. So not at all like the other dominoes, a double can never turn a corner.

The shape or form of the domino chain creates snake-line aimlessly as indicated by the impulses of the players and the limitations that come with the playing surface.

Beginning with a shuffle with the flat of the hand, the dominoes are face down in circles, making an appealing sound that has been well-known for generations. Each participant receives a predetermined quantity of dominoes, which varies depending on the number of players. Up to four players each receive 15 dominoes, five or six players each receive 12 dominoes, and seven or eight players each receive 10 dominoes.

In casual games, players usually only arrange their dominoes on the edge of the table in a row facing each other. The dominoes that are left are referred to as sleeping tiles or "the boneyard.

To begin, each player chooses a slot on the outer edge of the table that is facing them, which will serve as the starting point for their train. The hub is placed in the center of the table, and each player chooses a slot on the outer edge of the table that is facing them, which will serve as the starting point for their train.

It is decided that one additional slot will be used as the starting point for the 'Mexican Train,' and a Mexican Train marker is placed in this slot to signal that it is the starting point.

The order at which the tiles have been laid on the board or table is simply known as the line of play. It often begins with a single tile and grows in opposite directions as players add matching tiles. In practice, players frequently play tiles at right angles when the line of play approaches the table's edge.

The rules governing the line of play frequently alter between variants. The doubles act as spinners in many rules, as they can be played on all four sides, forcing the line of play to branch. The first tile of play, which acts as the primary spinner, must times be a double. Certain games, such as Chicken Foot, require that all sides of a spinner be occupied before anybody else may play. Matador's matching rules are peculiar. Due to the curved nature of the tiles in Bendomino, one or both sides of the line of play may be obstructed for geometrical reasons.

The game of Mexican Train, as well as other train games, begins with a spinner from which numerous trains branch off. The majority of trains are owned by players, and in most cases, players are only permitted to expand their own train.

A games of double 12 Mexican train dominoes can run anywhere from two to three hours. It all depends on the version you're playing, how many players are playing, and how long each player takes to think about and play their hand.

A game of double 12 Mexican Dominoes takes roughly 3 hours to play with 5 players.

The Mexican Train Dominoes Rules And Regulations

The version of the rules for Mexican Train Dominoes that Masters Traditional Games believes to be the most straightforward, elegant, and which minimizes the chance of repetitive or tedious elements of play. These should be simple to pick up, but they should still include all of the elements that are required for traditional Mexican Train Dominoes.

Bosses Traditional Games has given beneath the form of the guidelines to Mexican Train Dominoes that we accept are the most clear, rich and which limit the opportunity of monotonous or dull components of play. These ought to be anything but difficult to adapt yet contain the entirety of the essential elements for exemplary Mexican Train

Dominoes. In rundown, we think our variant of the guidelines are the best time!

Mexican Train Equipment

Mexican Train Dominoes are played with a standard arrangement of Double 12 dominoes. Each set has 91 dominoes and we suggest that dominoes with colored spots are utilized on the grounds that else it gets hard to coordinate with dominoes initially.

In contrast to most other kinds of dominoes, Mexican Train requires some other gear or equipment. First and foremost, a unique hub is utilized that has a space in the center for the beginning double and 8 openings around its edge to begin every domino train. Centers range from costly made things that go 'Toot Toot' when squeezed to home-put forth attempts that a few minutes to remove from a piece of cardboard.

Besides, two sorts of marker are needed for the game. These can be anything other than coins are usually utilized - say a penny for every player's train and a 20 pence coin or a 'nickel' for the Mexican Train. Sets explicitly advertised for the play of Mexican Train Dominoes ordinarily have distinctively shaded minimal plastic trains that are utilized to check every player's train.

A regular set of Double Twelve dominoes is required in order to play a game of Mexican Train Dominoes. If you don't use dominoes with colored spots, it can be difficult to match up dominoes at a glance, so each set comes with 91 dominoes. We recommend using dominoes with colored spots.

Mexican Train is a domino game that, in contrast to the vast majority of other domino games, calls for additional components. In the beginning, a specialized hub is used. This hub has a slot in the middle for the starting double and eight slots around its edge for beginning each domino train. There is a diverse selection of hubs on the market, ranging from inexpensive homemade versions that can be cut out of a piece of cardboard in a matter of minutes to more expensive commercially produced varieties that produce a "Toot Toot" noise when pressed.

Second, there are two distinct kinds of markers that are needed for the game. These can be anything, but coins are the most common choice; for example, each player's train is given a penny, and the Mexican Train is given a 20-pence coin, also known as a "nickel." Sets that have been designed and manufactured expressly for the game of Mexican Train Dominoes typically come with a set of plastic trains in a variety of colors that are used to mark which train belongs to which player.

Types of Mexican Train Dominoes

Two players (start with 8 tiles), three players (start with 6 tiles), five players (start with 5 tiles), or four players without affiliation can all play in the same way.

A similar game can be played with a twofold twelve set (91 tiles) or a twofold nine set (55 tiles) domino sets. With a twofold twelve set, four players would pick 12 tiles each and with a twofold nine set, nine tiles would be taken toward the beginning.

The Draw Game

Actually close to a variation of the Block game, the Draw Game is more mainstream in numerous pieces of the world. Players take less Mexican Train Dominoes at first however a player who can't put a domino should pick a resting domino to add to their set. At the point when the dozing Mexican Train Dominoes run out, players just pass their turn when they can't go. For this variety, two players would begin with 7 Mexican Train Dominoes, three players with 5 tiles, four players with 4 tiles and five players with 3 tiles.

The contrast between the two games is that in the Draw Game, players realize that all the tiles will wind up in play - this empowers them to more readily reason what tiles different players may be holding. With the Block game, since a couple of tiles stay resting and obscure all through the game, a bigger component of vulnerability rules.

Cross Mexican Train Dominoes

An augmentation to the Draw game, this variety gives players more choices and furthermore occupies less table room!

The game is played in the very same manner as the Draw game yet with an alternate beginning. After the principal doublet is played, the following four tiles played should be played against that doublet in order to frame a cross. So for this first doublet just, Mexican Train Dominoes are played adjoining every one of the four sides of the tile. Players may need to take dozing tiles before this is cultivated however when the cross is finished, play proceeds as in the draw game. Along these lines starting there on, each turn has four Mexican Train Dominoes accessible to be played against rather than two.

Twofold Nine Cross Mexican Train Dominoes

This variety is reasonable for Double Nine sets. A few players start with seven tiles every, at least four players start with five tiles each. Play begins according to Cross Mexican Train Dominoes with the second to fifth tiles played shaping a cross around the underlying doublet. From there on play proceeds according to the Draw game yet at whatever point a doublet is set down, two new chains can begin from it. Consequently, the quantity of accessible chains turns out to be a lot bigger than for past games.

Similar game beginning with similar number of tiles per individual ought to be conceivable with Double Twelve sets, as well.

Each of the Fives

Otherwise called "Muggins" and "The Five Game", All Fives is played with a twofold six arrangement of Mexican Train Dominoes by two to four players. The Mexican Train Dominoes are rearranged face down and every player takes five Mexican Train Dominoes (paying little mind to the quantity of players). The player with the most elevated doublet plays first and turns continue a clockwise way. Scoring occurs during and toward the finish of each game so it is critical to keep track continually - a cribbage board is an ideal scoring apparatus.

The primary player sets out any tile and play proceeds as in the Block Game with every player setting out a tile so the tile it associates with matches in number. Players furthermore endeavor to set down tiles so the amount of the numbers at one or the flip side of the chain amount to 5 or a numerous of 5 in light of the fact that any such play adds that add up to the score of the player. Doublets are set down across the course of the chain as in the Block game and for the reasons adding up to the two closures consider the complete of all spots on the doublet. Thus, for example, if there is a 3 toward one side of the chain and a 6 at the other, a player could play the twofold 6 which would be helpful in light of the fact that the finishes would amount to 3 + 6 + 6 = 15, a different of five. On the off chance that there is a twofold five toward one side and a clear at the other, a player could play the twofold clear so the finishes amount to 10.

While there are at least three resting tiles left in the center of the table, when a player can't play, that player takes a dozing tile all things considered. Once there are just two dozing tiles remaining, a player who can't play only passes for that turn.

The game finishes when a player has no more tiles left or on the other hand when none of the players can play a tile. The victor is the player who has no tiles left or, if no player figured out how to go out, the players include the spots on their excess Mexican Train Dominoes and the champ is the player with the littlest aggregate. Every failure deducts the victor's spot absolute (which is zero if the champ went out) from their spot complete, adjusts the outcome to the closest numerous of five and adds this amount to the score of the champ. For instance, if the champ has a spot all out of 3, and the washouts have separately spot aggregates of 11, 6 and 5, the complete granted to the victor is determined as follows:

Failure 1 takes away the champ's spot complete of 3 from 11 = 8 and rounds this to the closest numerous of 5 which is 10.

Washout 2 deducts the champ's spot all out of 3 from 6 = 3 and rounds this to the closest various of 5 which is 5.

Failure 3 takes away the victor's spot absolute of 3 from 5 = 2 and rounds this to the closest various of 5 which is 0.

So the champ acquires 15 additional focuses.

The primary player to arrive at a score of 100 dominates the game.

Every one of the Fives and Threes

This game is played similarly as All Fives aside from that products of three presently additionally mean focuses. So during the game, if a player sets out a tile with the end goal that the closures amount to 6, that players scores 6 focuses for the various of 3. An aggregate of 10 scores 10 focuses for a various of five and a sum of 15 scores 15 focuses (a numerous of five and three). Toward the finish of the game, the victor is basically granted the focuses from the failures remaining tiles or their disparities on a point for point premise.

Rearranging the Tiles

Before each game, a player rearranges the tiles face down on a level playing surface, altogether blending them by moving them in with his hands. The player's hands may not remain on similar tiles while rearranging, and the player who does the rearranging ought to be the last to draw his hand for the game.

Players may decide to alternate rearranging before each game or a similar player may rearrange the Mexican Train Dominoes before each game.

Here are two of a few choices: 1) The player to one side of the player making the primary play does the rearranging for a game; or, 2) The victor of the past game mixes for the following game.

How To Play Mexican Train Dominoes

Preparation For The Game

To begin, the dominoes are flattened out with the palm of the hand and shuffled in circles, producing an enticing sound that has been well-known for centuries. The number of dominoes that each player draws is predetermined and determined by the total number of players. Up to four players take 15 dominoes each, five or six players take 12 dominoes each, and seven or eight players take 10 dominoes each.

When playing dominoes with friends, players typically just line up their pieces on edge in a row in front of them. The dominoes that are still in play are referred to as "sleeping" tiles or "the boneyard."

The hub is positioned in the center of the table, and each player chooses a slot on the table's perimeter that is facing them to serve as the beginning point for the train they are controlling.

It is decided that one additional slot will serve as the beginning point for the "Mexican Train," and the marker for the "Mexican Train" is then placed in this slot to indicate that this is the case.

The Mexican Train Hub is moved to the player who has the highest double and is placed there by that player.

Arrangement

To start, the dominoes are rearranged face down around and around with the level of the hand - creating an alluring sound that has been notable for quite a long time. Contingent upon the quantity of players, every player draws a set number of dominoes. Up to 4 players take 15 dominoes every, 5 or 6 take 12 every, 7 or 8 take 10 each.

In benevolent games, players ordinarily place their dominoes anxious straight confronting them. The leftover dominoes are named "resting" tiles or "the boneyard".

The center is set in the table and every player chooses a space on the external edge that is confronting them to be the beginning stage for their train.

One extra opening is picked to be the beginning stage for the 'Mexican Train' and the Mexican Train marker is set in this space to indicate it thusly.

The player with the most noteworthy twofold places it in the focal point of the Mexican Train Hub.

The First Turn

The player to the left hand side of the player who put down the most elevated double beginnings and players then, at that point alternate turns in a direction that is clockwise.

The very first turn that a player makes at Mexican Train Dominoes is diverse to resulting turns and can require some idea to give the best benefit.

The player begins their 'train' by placing their initial domino into their selected slot on the center hub. The end pointing towards the center should coordinate with the focal center point domino. They then, at that point keep on broadening this 'train' by adding more dominoes from their hand until they can put down no more.

The Start

Every player draws 6 Mexican Train Dominoes and spots them with the goal that different players can't see their worth. The customary English bar technique for doing this is face down in two lines of three so each of the six can be gotten with two hands, taken a gander at and returned leaving the other hand free for the similarly significant business of drinking a half quart. Amateurs can simply put them on their edge straight confronting them. Remaining Mexican Train Dominoes are named "dozing" tiles.

The primary individual to play is that individual holding the twofold six, or bombing that the twofold five, etc. The tile played should be the twofold tile that allowed the player to take the primary turn. On the off chance that none of the players hold a twofold, at that point the tiles are reshuffled and re-drawn.

Every player should thusly then play a tile onto the table situating it with the goal that it contacts one finish of the domino chain which accordingly slowly increments long.

In the event that a player plays a domino with the outcome that the two finishes of the chain show a similar number (typically a number which is helpful to the player and tacky to the rivals), that player is said to have "sewed up" the closures.

How the tiles are put gives a little piece of the diversion. Each tile being put should be situated with the goal that the two coordinating finishes are adjoining. Except if, the tile is a twofold, the tile can be set square in any of the three bearings as long as the two coordinating sides are contacting completely. Pairs are constantly positioned cross-ways across the finish of the chain. A tile played to a twofold should likewise be set as needs be - opposite to the twofold contacting at its center. The state of the domino chain creates snake-line indiscriminately as indicated by the impulses of the players and the constraints of the playing surface.

On the off chance that a player can lay a domino, at that point it should be played. In any case the player "thumps", or raps the table and play passes to the following player. The rival players will, obviously, give careful consideration of the numbers presently accessible on the table and attempt to guarantee that they are accessible in future too.....

Ordinarily play stops when one player "chips out" (plays his last domino) albeit a few renditions require the two accomplices to chip out. On the off chance that it arrives at a point where no player can continue, the champs are the accomplices whose consolidated amount of all spots on their leftover Mexican Train Dominoes is the least.

For scoring, a few bars would play a point for each game. An all the more fascinating strategy, that may be scored utilizing a cribbage board, has the victors score the amount of all spots on the washouts remaining tiles. In a game which doesn't bring about anybody chipping out, the victors would get the contrast between the champs all out spots and the washouts absolute spots. A game can be played to 100 focuses, state, or on a cribbage board, 121 focuses.

The Very First Twist

The round begins with the player to the left of the player who placed the highest double, and players then take turns moving in a clockwise direction around the table.

When playing Mexican Train Dominoes, each player's first turn is unique in comparison to subsequent turns, and determining how to use it to their advantage may require some careful consideration.

The 'train' that the player is building is kicked off when they place their first domino into the space of their choice on the hub. It is necessary for the end that is pointing toward the middle to coincide with the central hub domino. They then proceed to add more dominoes from their hand in order to extend this "train" until they are unable to set any more dominoes down.

Subsequent Turns

Each subsequent turn, a player is only allowed to place one domino on any of the trains that are available to that player, regardless of which train that domino is placed on. The maneuver is carried out in the following manner:

If the player is still unable to participate in the game, they must place a marker on the domino that represents the final domino in their train. This opens up the player's train so that it can be used by any of the other players.

At each resulting turn, a player can put down just a single domino on any of the trains that are accessible to that player. The turn continues as follows:

1. If conceivable, the player plays a domino to one of the accessible trains (see underneath) and that is the finish of the turn.

2. Otherwise, the player takes a domino from the boneyard. On the off chance that it's conceivable, the new domino from the boneyard is played to one of the accessible trains (see beneath) and that is the finish of the turn.

3. If the player actually can't play, then, at that point the player puts a marker on the domino toward the finish of their train, consequently making that player's train accessible for the wide range of various player's to utilize.

At whatever point a player plays a domino to their own train, if their train has a marker on it, the marker is then taken out.

Assuming a player plays a Double, that player promptly has another turn.

Available Trains

Any of the accompanying trains are accessible to the player:

• The player's own train.

• The Mexican Train (if not yet began, the player can begin the train with a domino coordinating with the middle Double).

• Another player's train however just in the event that it is having a marker on it.

Winning

The objective of the game is to be the first player to empty your hand of all of the dominoes in your possession. The game is over as soon as this occurs, regardless of whether or not the final tile is a Double.

The player who wins receives a score of zero, while the other players add up the total number of spots on the dominoes they still have in their hands to determine their score.

In most cases, a series of games will be played, and the winner of the match will be determined by which player finishes the series with the fewest points.

Special Situations

In the extremely unlikely event that no player has a double in their hand to begin the game, players will take turns picking cards from the boneyard until someone selects a double, at which point the double will be placed in the hub immediately.

Because there won't be enough room on the hub for the Mexican Train if there are 8 players, the game will have to begin with the Mexican Train off by itself, some distance from the hub.

In the extremely unlikely event that one player uses up all of their dominoes during their first turn, the remaining players are given the opportunity to finish their first turns as well. The game is over and the points are tallied when all players have had a chance to take their first turn since the game began.

General Variations

Some players begin a match by placing the Double 12 domino on the table for the first game, followed by the Double 11 domino for the second game, and so on until the 13th and final game of the match, which begins with the Double blank domino.

In some variants of the game, the first turn is not treated differently from the other turns, and players are permitted to lay down the same number of tiles as they would on any other turn during their first turn.

Minor departure from Playing Doubles

There are a ton of expanded varieties for playing Doubles. Bosses Traditional Games doesn't suggest these principles for novices, youngsters or individuals favoring more clear play as they add additional unpredictability to the game and new circumstances that moderate the game down fairly.

The fundamental and most normal extra principle for Doubles play is that where a Double exists toward the finish of any train, the Double should then be 'fulfilled' (laid against) in the following turn, regardless of whether the Double is on another player's train that isn't stamped.

A minor departure from the above Doubles decide that a player who plays a Double and who hence has quickly has another turn, isn't for this reward go needed to play against a Double. The player can play against any accessible train. This obviously implies that a player can play a few Doubles in succession, so players throughout the following not many goes need to play against at least two Doubles before they can proceed in the more ordinary style.

Individuals playing the past variety, some of the time confound things further so that in the circumstance where at least two Doubles are played by one player, each Double must be played in the converse request that they were set down.

When playing the obligatory Double play rule, it can happen that a Double is set toward the finish of a train and that all dominoes to coordinate that Double have just been laid. This Double needs to then be overlooked starting there on (in any case the game would stop). A few people will at that point stack the twofold on the past tile of the train to show that the train has forever halted.

Domino Strategies For Mexican Trains

When you play a game as frequently as we have, you begin to notice certain patterns in how individuals play the game. Here are the three most effective tactics we employ to help us succeed.

Prepared & Organized: This is my (Kait's) technique! I line up my tiles on my tray and strive to make the longest train after picking up my tiles for a round. When you have many numbers that potentially line up, be careful to experiment with different combinations; you never know which combination will result in the longest train on your rack.

I put any dominoes that don't fit in my train at the bottom of my tray. When the round starts, I'll start by placing dominoes from my planned train on my rack on my train. I'll try to open up the "Mexican" train as soon as feasible if I have a lot of spare tiles that aren't part of my train. If I have an extra domino that can be placed on another train at any time, I will do it. The idea behind this is because I know I can get on my train with the dominoes I planned out at any time, so I want to get rid of the additional dominoes as soon as possible.

Only when I don't have a domino to close a double will I not add an extra domino on another train!!! This is simply too dangerous for me; if I set a double down without a domino to back it up, I am compelled to pick one from the spare pile. If I'm lucky, it'll match the number I need, but if it doesn't, I'll have to open up my train to the other players, which will effectively demolish my intended train.

Risk It Chaos. This is Branden's Mexican Train Dominoes Strategy. Branden relies on taking risks and producing chaos to win, despite the fact that he utilizes some structure by setting out his train ahead of time.

Sneaky and High Roller. In this approach, you start by arranging your train tiles on the rack in such a way that other players can't determine how many tiles you have on your starting train. Make up bogus breaks so they don't believe you're on a continuous train. This has the potential to throw them off.

This method focuses on how you put out your tiles at the start. When it comes to setting out your tiles, you may find that you have several possibilities. If there are numerous possibilities, always try to use the tiles with the highest number first. Remember that at the end of the game, the player with the lowest score wins. As a result, keep an eye on your higher tiles throughout the game. If you have the option to remove a higher tile at any moment, do so.

Create a train with fewer tiles yet higher scores. When constructing your train, don't get caught up on the number of tiles. Rather, concentrate on the higher points and, if possible, place them at the beginning of your train. Because the round may finish before you are able to get rid of all of your tiles, getting rid of higher score tiles is critical. If you're left with low-scoring tiles at the conclusion of the game, you're probably going to win.

Contesting At Mexican Train Dominoes

1-Remove the set's double-12 or double-9 dominoes.

For a 13-hand game, use a domino set with a double-12; for a 10-hand game, choose a double-9 set. Remove the highest double-sided tile from whichever set you pick before shuffling.

The game of Mexican Train begins with the highest double-sided tile in the center of the table. Each subsequent hand begins with the double-sided tile that is one less than the previous hand: the first hand begins with the double-12, the second hand begins with the double-11, the third hand begins with the double-10, and so on.

2 - Shuffle the rest of the dominoes facedown on the table in front of you.

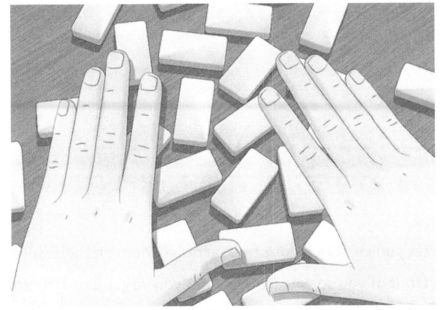

Arrange all of the tiles and flip them over so that the pip-side is facing down. By hand, thoroughly mix them up.

Because Mexican Train features so many rounds, have players take turns flipping and shuffling the tiles.

3-Draw cards from the shuffled tiles for each player.

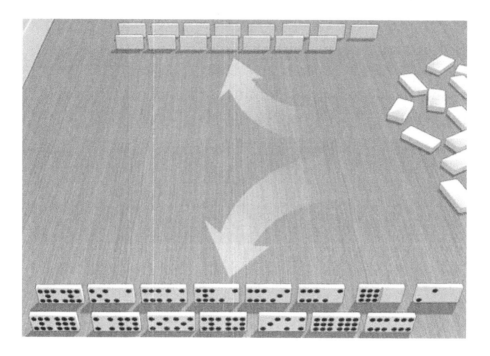

After you've drawn your tiles, arrange them on their sides in front of you so you can see what you've got, but attempt to keep them hidden from your neighbors. If you have a double-12 set, you can play Mexican train with up to eight people. If you own a double-9 set, you can play with as little as two to four players. Determine how many tiles each person should take using the following breakdown:

Double-12: 2 to 3 players each take 16 tiles; 4 players each take 15 tiles; 5 players each take 14 tiles; 6 players each take 12 tiles; 7 players each take 10 tiles; 8 players each take 9 tiles.

Double-9: Two players receives 15 tiles; three players receive 13 tiles; and four players receive 10 tiles.

4 -Place the remaining tiles in the "train yard" for future draws.

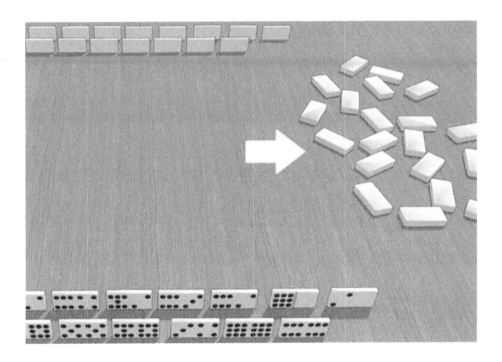

If you do not have a domino in your hand that may be played on the Mexican train or your personal train during any given turn, draw one tile from the train yard. If a tile is playable, play it. If you do not, the card is added to your hand and the turn is passed to the next player.

The "train yard" is occasionally referred to as the "bone pile."

Maintain an upright position for the tiles in the train yard.

5 -To begin, place the double domino in the center of the table.

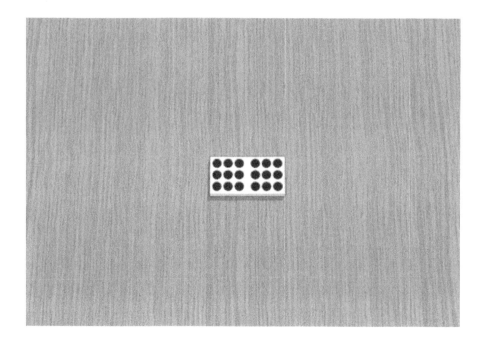

After designing tiles for your hand and building the train yard, the game may finally begin! There are certain sets available that contain a small stand for the starter tile, which you may use if you have one. Otherwise, simply center the double-12 or double-9 tile in the playing space.

The starter tile is frequently called the "engine tile".

Everybody can play off the engine tile, but each player's personal train is not fair game for other players unless it contains a marker, which occurs when a player is unable to perform their turn.

6 –Choose someone to begin and go turns clockwise around the table.

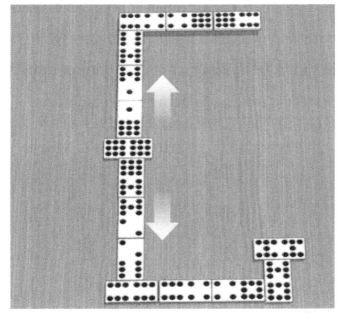

Whoever goes first may place a tile only if it is the same denomination as the engine tile. If the engine tile is a double-12, for example, you must lay down a tile with 12 pips on one or both sides. The 12-pip side must be set down parallel to the double-12 engine tile.

The exception to the one tile per turn rule is if you place a double tile, which means that the pips on both sides of the tile are identical/same. If you place a double tile, immediately take a second turn and place an additional tile.

Utilizing a Marker: If you are unable to take a turn after drawing a tile from the train yard, place a small marker on your train, such as a dime. This implies that other players can now play both on your train and independently. To remove the marker, you must play a tile on your personal train, at which point it reverts to being entirely yours.

7-Be the first to lay down all of your dominoes to win a hand.

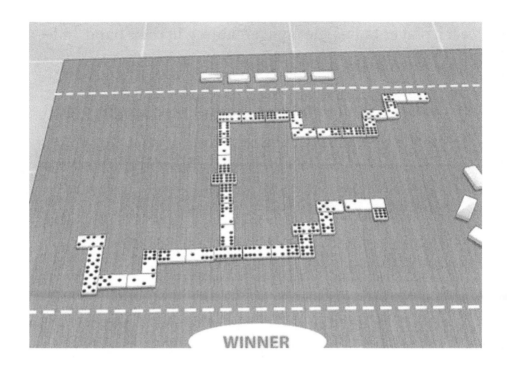

WINNER

Once a player has placed all of the tiles in their hand, the round is complete. Record the score on a piece of paper; have each player with remaining tiles sum up the total amount of pips. Add this number below their name on the scoresheet. The objective is to have the lowest figure at the conclusion of all rounds.

A set of double-12 dominoes will comprise thirteen rounds, while a set of double-9 dominoes will contain ten.

The other only way for a round to end is if the whole train yard is depleted and no one can move. In that instance, each player tallies the pips remaining in their hand and adds them to the score sheet.

8 -Continue to play and keep track of your progress until all double tiles have been used.

Each new round begins with an engine tile that is one number less than the previous hand's (double-9 for the first hand, double-8 for the second hand, double-7 for the third, and so on). The blank double is the final engine you'll use before the game's conclusion (blank tiles can only be matched with tiles that also have a blank side).

When you shuffle between rounds, the previously used double tiles are just blended back in with the other tiles.

Chapter 3: Different Approaches To Playing Dominoes

How to play The Game Of Doubles

When it comes to playing doubles, there are a ton of extended variations available. These rules are not recommended by Masters Traditional Games for players new to the game, children, or anyone who enjoys a more straightforward style of play because they add an additional layer of complexity to the game as well as new circumstances that slightly slow down the pace of play.

If there is a double at the end of any train, that double has to be "satisfied" (played against) on the next player's turn. This is true even if the double is on another player's train that has not been marked for play. This is the fundamental and most common additional rule for playing Doubles. If a player is unable to play against the Double immediately or after drawing from the Boneyard, they are required to place a marker on their train and the turn then passes to the player to their left. All other available trains are disregarded in this scenario. In a normal game, this rule would not be in effect during the first round of the special game.

A variation on the Doubles rule described above states that a player who plays a Double and who consequently has another turn immediately afterward is exempt from the requirement that they play against a Double during their bonus turn. The game can be played against any train that is currently available. This, of course, denotes that a player is able to play multiple Doubles in a row, which means that players on the subsequent few turns will need to face off against two or more Doubles before they can proceed in a manner that is more typical.

People who play the variation that came before can sometimes make things more difficult by requiring that whenever one player plays two or more doubles, each double must be played in the opposite order in which it was laid down. This makes things more difficult for people who play that variation.

When following the mandatory Double play rule, it is possible for a Double to be placed at the end of a train after all of the dominoes that are necessary to match that Double have already been laid out. After that, it is imperative that this Double be disregarded going forward (otherwise the game would come to a halt). After that, some players will place the double on the tile that came before it on the train to denote that the train has come to a complete and permanent halt.

Step By Step Instructions To Play The Game

Dominos are played into the center by coordinating dominos along with a similar number. Play starts by coordinating one of your dominos with the center twofold domino number. Every player is permitted to play however many dominos as he/she needs on the main turn of a round.

The first round beginnings with the twofold 12. The second round beginnings with the twofold 11, etc down to the twofold zero beginning the last round. The starting twofold domino is set aside while players are drawing dominos. Players draw the accompanying measure of dominos dependent on the number of players are playing.

2-4 players: 15 dominos each

5-6 players: 12 dominos each

7-8 players: 10 dominos each

9-10 players: 8 dominos each

The additional dominos are pushed to the side to make the boneyard.

First turn

Starting with the beginning player and proceeding with clockwise, a domino or line of dominoes known as the player's "train" is assembled emerging from the train center towards the player. This train should have an end coordinating the motor in the focal point of the train center. For instance, if the motor in the train center is a twofold 12, the train should start with a 12 on the beginning end. The train can be any measure of dominoes inasmuch as every domino in the train has a coordinating finish to the adjoining domino.

Coordinating Dominoes

Dominoes with indistinguishable closures can be put corresponding to one another to save space insofar as they don't hinder any other individual's train. This is known as "bowing" the train and is altogether discretionary. In the event that there is a "twofold" (a tile with an equivalent measure of pips or same number on the two closures) on the train, it is set opposite to the contiguous domino.

Public Train

Note: If a player closes his train in a twofold on the main turn, everybody keeps completing their first go as indicated by the guidelines. In any case, on the second turn players must "fulfill" the twofold (as clarified in the Playing Doubles segment) before some other kind of play can be made.

Fulfilling the Double

Public Trains

A train that is set apart with a train token is public and any player can add to that train after it is set apart, besides during the main turn. A train that isn't stamped is "private" and just the player who began that train can add to it. A player who has denoted their train public may change their train back to a private train and eliminate the marker in ensuing turns in the event that they can play a coordinating end.

Ensuing Turns

After everybody has played their first turn, beginning with the primary player, every player adds to their train or a public train from their hand. In contrast to the principal turn, players can just add each domino in turn.

On the off chance that the player can't add a domino, the player should draw a domino from the boneyard and play that domino promptly in the event that he can. If not, he should check his train public. Anytime in the game, if there are no more tiles in the boneyard to draw, the player basically denotes his train public.

In the event that There Are No More Dominoes in the Boneyard

Playing Doubles

On the off chance that a player plays a "twofold", the twofold should be put opposite to the train played on. The player should then promptly play another domino from his hand on to the twofold subsequently "fulfilling the twofold", or on to any open trains.

In the event that the player completes his chance without fulfilling the twofold, the accompanying player has the commitment to fulfill that twofold. On the off chance that that player can't fulfill the twofold from his hand, he should draw from the boneyard and fulfill the twofold with that domino. In the event that he can't, the player denotes his own train public and afterward the commitment to fulfill the twofold proceeds on the accompanying players as indicated by similar guidelines.

On the off chance that an overabundance to be fulfilled, they should be fulfilled according to the pattern in which they showed up in play.

Mexican Train

An uncommon "Mexican Train" might be begun by any player with a domino from their hand that has a coordinating end with the motor. It reaches out of the motor and is constantly stamped public and never gets private. It stays separate from every close to home train.

The Mexican Train might be begun any turn with the exception of the primary turn, or on a turn where a twofold should be fulfilled.

Just a single Mexican Train might be made for any round.

How to play Block Game

The simplest domino version takes two players and a double-6 set. Shuffle the 28 tiles face down to create the boneyard.

Seven tiles are drawn from the boneyard by each participant. Once the players have begun drawing tiles, the tiles are often placed on their edges in front of them to enable every player see their own tile, but not to see the value of the tiles drawn by the other players when they have finished placing their own tiles. As a result, at any time throughout the game, each player can see how many tiles their opponent still has in his or her hands.

When someone inquires as to whether or not you know how to play dominoes, this is most often the first game that comes to mind.

Because it is so straightforward and easy to understand, it is a fantastic game to begin playing with little experience.

The number of participants is as follows:

2–4 players are required.

The Equipment consists of the following:

A set of dominoes with a Double-Six configuration. In addition, there is a mechanism to keep score.

The Preparation:

Each participant takes a turn drawing a domino to determine who goes first. The tile with the greatest weight wins.

Put the dominoes in a shuffle and distribute 7 dominoes to each participant in a two-handed game, and 5 dominoes to each player in a three-or four-handed game.

Place the remaining tiles to the side of the playing area, away from the action.

The Block Game is typically played in a cutthroat fashion, but if you choose, you can play with partners to make it a four-handed game.

In the event that you are playing with a partner, make certain that your buddy is sitting across the table from you at the table.

The Scoring System:

If you're playing a cutthroat game, you'll want to be the player who has the lowest value of dominoes left in his hand at the end of the round.

When playing games with a partner, the entire worth of both partners' contributions is put together to determine who is the round's winner.

The winner obtains a point total equal to the sum of the values of all of their opponents' dominoes minus their own points earned during the game.

When playing with partners, cutthroat games are typically played to 61 points, whereas when playing alone, winners need 100 or more points.

The Most Common Variations are as follows:

The player with the greatest value is the first to double play.

The winner of the previous round will take the lead in the following round.

Beginning with a varied number of dominoes for each player, the round will be more interesting.

If the last domino is any double, or if the final domino could have been played at either end of the train, the points granted to the winner are doubled.

The Fundamental Strategy is as follows:

Lead with your strongest suit if you are playing with a group of people, preferably the two-card trick.

Attempt to conclude your turn with the ends of the train exhibiting suits that you have control over at the end of your round.

Make a note of the ends of the train as your opponents pass through.

Throughout the game, players earn points for various configurations, actions, and emptying their hands. The majority of scoring games employ variants of the draw game. A player must pick up an additional domino if he or she does not call "domino" prior to laying the tile on the table and another player says "domino" after the tile has been laid by the first player.

Scoring occurs at the conclusion of a blocking game. Following a player's completion of their hand, which results in the team winning the game, the score is determined based on the pip count of the losing team's hands. The pip count of the remaining boneyard is added in some regulations. When a game is halted due to an inability of a player to move, the winner is frequently determined by totaling the pips in the players' hands.

An "end" occurs when one of the players is eliminated, that is, when they have used all of their tiles. If no player is able to empty their hand, the player holding the lowest domino is declared out and receives one point. A game consists of an unlimited number of ends, with points earned in each end adding up to a total.

How to play Double Nine Cross Dominoes

This variety is reasonable for Double Nine sets. A few players start with seven tiles every, at least four players start with five tiles each. Play begins according to Cross dominoes with the second to fifth tiles played shaping a cross around the underlying doublet. From there on play proceeds according to the Draw game however at whatever point a doublet is set down, two new chains can begin from it. Hence, the quantity of accessible chains turns out to be a lot bigger than for past games.

Similar game beginning with similar number of tiles per individual ought to be conceivable with Double Twelve sets, as well.

Draw Game

In a draw game (blocking or scoring), players may draw as many tiles from the boneyard as they choose before playing a tile, and they are not permitted to pass until the boneyard is (almost) empty.

Both games can be adapted to accommodate more than two players, who can compete alone or in teams.

In the event that the boneyard is unfilled and a player can't play, that player's turn is skipped.

At the point when a player with an open train plays on another player's open train, his own train stays open. A train is possibly shut when played on by its proprietor.

A twofold should be played on before some other dominos are played.

Every player gets in any event one turn regardless of whether a player can play every one of his dominos on the principal turn. When all the players have taken their first turn, the score is refreshed dependent on every player's unplayed dominos.

How To Play All Fives or Muggins Dominoes

All Fives is played with a twofold six arrangement of dominoes by two to four players. The dominoes are rearranged face down and every player takes five dominoes (paying little heed to the amount of players). The player with the most elevated doublet plays first and turns continue a clockwise way. Scoring occurs during and toward the finish of each game so it is imperative to keep track continually - a cribbage board is an ideal scoring instrument.

The 1st player sets out any tile and play proceeds as in the Block Game with every player setting out a tile so the tile it associates with matches in number. Players moreover endeavor to set down tiles so the amount of the numbers at one or the flip side of the chain amount to 5 or a various of 5 on the grounds that any such play adds that add up to the score of the player. Doublets are set down across the heading of the chain as in the Block game and for the reasons adding up to the two finishes consider the absolute of all spots on the doublet. Thus, for example, if there is a 3 toward one side of the chain and a 6 at the other, a player could play the twofold (double) 6 which would be valuable on the grounds that the finishes would amount to $3 + 6 + 6 = 15$, a different of five.

In a situation where a player set out a tile with the goal that the closures amount to a multiple of five and neglect to proclaim it, any of the player can yell "Muggins!" when the following tile is laid and guarantee the score all things considered. While there are at least three resting tiles left in the center of the table, when a player can't play, that player takes a sleeping tile all things considered. Once there are just two dozing tiles staying, a player who can't play simply passes for that turn.

The game finishes when a player has no more tiles left or on the other hand when none of the players can play a tile. The victor is the player who has no tiles left or, if no player figured out how to go out, the players include the spots on their leftover dominoes and the champ is the player with the least total. Every failure takes away the victor's spot complete (which is zero if the champ went out) from their spot absolute, adjusts the outcome to the closest various of five and adds this amount to the score of the champ. For instance, if the champ has a spot with a total of 3, and the losers have separately spot aggregates of 11, 6 and 5, the overall total granted to the victor is determined as follows:

• Loser 1 deducts the champ's spot a total of 3 is deducted from 11 = 8 and rounds this to the closest different of 5 which is 10.

• Loser 2 takes away the champ's spot all out of 3 from 6 = 3 and rounds this to the closest various of 5 which is 5.

• Loser 3 deducts the champ's spot total of 3 from 5 = 2 and rounds this to the closest different of 5 which is 0.

So the victor acquires 15 additional points.

The 1st competitor to arrive at a score of 100 dominates the game.

Game of Muggins is a very popular scoring game in which players attempt to complete their turns by having the total value at both ends of the train be at least a multiple of 5.

The number of participants is as follows:

2–4 players are required.

The Equipment consists of the following:

A Double-Six set of dominoes, as well as an easy way to keep track of the points earned. Although a cribbage board makes scoring easier, a pencil and paper will function almost as well as a cribbage board.

The Preparation:

Each participant takes a turn drawing a domino to determine who goes first. The tile with the greatest weight wins.

Put the dominoes in a shuffle and distribute 7 dominoes to each participant in a two-handed game, and 5 dominoes to each player in a three-or four-handed game.

The remainder of the tiles is placed in the bone yard, where they are easily accessible to all players. Muggins is always shown as a ruthless thug.

The Script for the Play:

The player in the lead places a tile of his choosing on the field.

All doubles are set vertically, and the entire value of both ends of doubles is used for calculating the score for a pair of doubles. The first double is the only one that can be spun.

If the first tile scores, the player's turn is over and the tile is marked down. The person to the left can now place a tile on either end of the board that has the same number of places as the tile on the other end.

Keep track of any points earned during the game.

To avoid drawing dominoes from the bone yard, players must wait until they are able to set down a domino on their turn before drawing another from it.

It is possible to be stopped from drawing or laying down dominoes, in which case the player must pass without scoring any points for the turn.

The game continues until one player has dominoed all of the other players or until no one can make a legitimate move.

The Scoring System:

Players can score points by concluding their turn with the open ends of the layout adding up to a number greater than or equal to five, as seen in the illustration (5, 10, 15, 20, etc.).

The player receives points in an amount equal to the total. When a player completes his turn with a total of five points on the ends, he will immediately receive five points in addition to his previous score.

If the player's points earned during the game allow him or her to reach the required number of points to win, the game is declared a success.

The points are then awarded to the player who has won the round in question.

A two-handed game when the losing player has three dominoes left in his hand, 1-2, 2-6, and 0-1, results in the winning player receiving 15 points: 1-2 rounds up to 5, 2-6 rounds up to 10, and 0-1 rounds down to 0.

Head-to-head games are normally played to a maximum of 250 points, whereas other games are played to a maximum of 200 points.

For those who like to keep score using a cribbage board, each hole is worth five points.

The Most Common Variations are as follows:

It is against the rules to draw any additional tiles.

In a two-handed game, this means not drawing the last two tiles from the bone yard, or the last tile if there are more persons playing.

There has been a change in the number of points required to win.

The Fundamental Strategy is as follows:

Start with the 5-5 or a scoring tile to establish a strong foundation.

Keep the ends of the layout as low as possible, particularly if your opponent is on the verge of victory.

Play more aggressively early in each round, attempting to score points as soon as possible.

In the later phases of the game, you should play more defensively, seeking to block your opponent's shots.

How to play All Fives and Threes

This game is played similarly as All Fives aside from that products of three currently likewise mean points. So during the game, if a player sets out a tile to such an extent that the finishes amount to 6, that players scores 6 points for the different of 3. A sum of 10 scores 10 points for a various of five and a sum of 15 scores 15 points (a different of five and three). Toward the finish of the game, the victor is essentially granted the points from the washouts remaining tiles or their disparities on a point for point premise.

How To Play Cuban Dominoes

Aside from baseball, the national pleasure in Cuba is playing dominoes.

Using a Double-Nine set, which is the most popular type of set in Hispanic countries, you can play this straightforward block game.

The number of participants is as follows:

4 players

The Equipment consists of the following:

A set of dominoes with a Double-Nine count. It's a way to keep track of things.

The Preparation:

Cuban Dominoes is a game that is played with a partner. In most cases, partners are picked at random using whatever manner that the players desire.

Partners must sit on the opposite side of the table from one another. Shuffle the dominoes and distribute 10 tiles to each player.

All of the remaining tiles should be removed from the playing area because they will not be used for the remainder of the game.

The Script for the Play:

The player who has the heaviest double is the first to lay down. In spite of the fact that doubles do not act as spinners, they are nonetheless played vertically.

The opponent to the right of the opener must either match or pass the end of the domino on which he or she is positioned.

When playing Cuban Dominoes, you have the option of passing even if you have a genuine play. It marks the end of the round when all four players have passed in a succession.

In order to obtain additional dominoes, there will be no drawing. Play proceeds in a counter-clockwise direction until someone dominoes or until everyone is prevented from making a lawful move by the opponent.

The opponents are then given his number, which serves as their score. A partnership is declared victorious when they reach a specific number of points at the end of a round of play.

Although 150 is usually considered to be the winning score, you can feel free to alter it to suit your needs and preferences.

The Most Common Variations are as follows:

Choosing who leads by selecting one domino from the pile of dominoes left over after the deal is complete. The heaviest domino is the first to fall.

Providing the winning team with the opportunity to open the following round.

Even if both pairs of partners achieve or exceed the winning number, the partners who are closest to the real number (the ones who have the lower total) are the ones that win the game.

The Fundamental Strategy is as follows:

Because your opponent's score is calculated depending on the value of the tiles in your hand at the end of the round, place your heaviest tiles on the table first to begin the game.

Keep track of the number of tiles of each level that are currently available. This will assist you in determining the strength of your opponent's hand.

Even if you have a legal play in front of you, you may wish to pass if you have relatively light dominoes and believe your opponents are blocked in order to obtain a larger score.

In addition to utilizing dominoes for competitive games, there are a variety of other methods to enjoy playing with them. In the 1800s, domino puzzles based on mathematics were a popular hobby in France.

Alternatively, if you find yourselves with a set of dominoes with no one to play against, you may try your hand at solitaire or practice toppling and stacking techniques.

People have even been known to utilize dominoes to predict the future!

Chapter 4: Dominoes Strategies And Tips

When playing Dominoes, you can apply a variety of techniques and approaches to maximize your chances of winning. All of which, the more you employ them during play, can offer you an advantage over your opponents.

The time has come to learn everything you can about dominoes, so let us get started.

Begin Your Doubles Matches Early

It is sensible and wise to simply begin with the doubles! There are typically fewer opportunities to play them because both sides have the identical suit values. This should be done early on to avoid being stuck with only doubles.

Apply the Winning Strategy

Set up your starting hand attempting to augment emptying the most tiles.

Set up the tiles start to finish. It's simplest to see with a tile rack.

In building your own train, consider that it very well may be ideal to construct a train with less tiles however with more focuses, particularly toward the front of the train. In the event that you play, you should quickly answer a twofold, there is a more prominent possibility you may need to separate your train to fulfill a twofold. On the off chance that you have high pip tiles at the rear of the train in your grasp, you may then make some harder memories playing those excess tiles.

Orchestrate the tiles in your grasp so that different players can only with significant effort tell the number of tiles you have in your train. Utilize counterfeit breaks to allow them to believe it's not nonstop.

Utilize the Mexican Train and other qualified trains to dump high-point tiles. While you may be slanted to focus on it to free your hand, everything being equal (counting depressed spot tiles) from the get-go in the round, hopefully accepting your train is a certain play, consider that you could be compelled to split it up to fulfill a twofold. This could leave you with high point tiles that are not a definite play!

At the point when you have a selection of plays, think about what conceivable favorable position or impediment your play will have for different players, particularly the individuals who are driving in the scoring. For instance, in the event that you play a twofold and can either fulfill it or play a non-twofold on another qualified train, consider which play will probably be generally great for you.

Since playing a twofold from any area in your own train doesn't separate the train, be available to playing it whenever it is playable.

Screen how close different players may be to finishing the round, and change your technique if necessary, e.g., on the off chance that you can play a twofold and leave it unsatisfied, they may be compelled to draw and put their markers on their trains.

Open duplicates should be fulfilled in the request they were played. In the event that you will play at least two pairs during your turn and you need to fulfill one of them to end your turn, play that twofold first.

On the off chance that you are committed to fulfill a twofold and you presume that each of the 13 tiles of the required group have just been played, tally before you draw, in case you superfluously obtain an additional tile.

Despite the fact that it's pleasant completion a round with your last tile, recollect: The low absolute score dominates the match. A lot of danger in attempting to end rounds can crush you eventually. On the off chance that you are holding low tiles and you don't go out, it doesn't make any difference.

A decent feign on your part may lead another player to settle on a helpless decision in play. Train is a great deal like poker, keep them speculating or you can generally gripe in any event, when you have a decent hand.

Your Biggest Tiles Go First

You should set your most heavily spotted tiles early in the game because it is difficult to anticipate who will win the game at the end.

First mover advantage

Being the first mover in the domino's game is always an advantage. Not just because you will have a bigger chance of finishing your cards first, but because it will help you control the game.

A first mover advantage is also a part of the Blue Ocean Strategy. The blue ocean strategy analytical model – with the practical tools it presents – offers a new and inspiring way to look at strategic innovation. It proposes techniques for developing new markets based on what proponents call value innovation – innovation linked to what buyers actually value.

The blue ocean model categorizes innovations as falling into either red or blue oceans.

Red ocean - The red ocean symbolizes the known market space. Red ocean strategies are for companies that want to brave the shark-infested waters crowded with both large entrenched companies and eager young companies. In the red oceans, rules and boundaries are defined and unquestioned and each entrant is trying to beat out its opponents for a larger share of the available business – a bigger piece of the pie.

Blue ocean - Blue oceans are the unknown market space. Companies that enter blue oceans simply avoid the predators altogether by diving in to the wide open areas. Unlike red oceans, blue oceans have untapped market space, allow demand creation, and have high growth and profit potential. Instead of trying to beat the competition as in red oceans, the competition is made irrelevant. Blue oceans are not defined by boundaries, rules, and limitations.

The only place that first-mover advantage doesn't work so well is in the technology sector. Here consumer behavior is often way behind technological breakthroughs. Sometimes the companies themselves are slow to realize the power of the technology at their fingertips. The rapid adoption of SMS messaging for example took most European mobile phone companies totally by surprise – so much so that many didn't even explain the facility in their instruction booklets.

Sudden Death Technique

Sudden death technique is one of the most famous and widely used techniques. It is used when you force the both sides of the cards to require a certain number that all its combinations are already on the play ground.

So when should you use this techniques? First you must make sure that you have both repeated numbers (More than three) and also a good combination. Second, make sure that the number of points you have is much less than those with your competitor as in the cases of sudden death games, the player with the less points wins.

A similar case in market is when companies force the market into a saturation zone. A high degree of imitation turns products into commodities, "permanent fixtures," attracting new entrants, especially in automobiles and electronics industries: "In industry after industry, bright ideas quickly become permanent fixtures.

Physiological war

Dominos is a perfect game to master the physiological mind manipulation games. Try to always comment on each move your competitor makes. Saying phrases like "Ha Ha, what an expected move", "Oh, you have just knocked yourself out", "Ha, You will regret such a move". Striking your cards strongly creating a boom sound on the playing board creates a sense of threatening within your competitor making him less concentrating on wining and more afraid of loosing.

Playing mind games with your competitor is not an easy task. You must in some cases prove that what you are saying is true and in minor cases just do not play hard to prove it. Again this helps you to avoid being expected. There is an old proverb says "To be known as powerful is as equal to being really powerful".

You're interested in winning and using power and influence, and for that you need a reputation as someone who uses power and has influence. It's hard to get noticed, and there are hundreds of people who like to be quiet achievers. Few of us want to be associated with

attributes like ruthlessness. But, when there's cruelty that needs to be done in the service of a greater good, your ability to continue to be a leader rests on 'whether cruel deeds are committed well or badly'.

Predict your competitor next move

Knowing what your rivals have in their minds is as equal as all the previous lessons together. By monitoring all their moves and analyzing them, you can have a semi clear picture of what they have in their hands and can predict their next move and their overall playing style. Some players for example tends to get rid of the cards with big numbers (5 & 6), or their SCC cards (66, 55, 44, 33, 22, 11, 00). These give you an idea that you playing with someone who is not a risk taker, he prefers to minimize his loss rather than taking a risk of wining. Other players tend to drag the game to a sudden death by throwing similar numbers to the board. Keeping attention to such patterns of playing helps you to predict the game direction and thus helping you get the most out of it.

Foreknowledge is very important in business world. There are big organizations that have complete dedicated teams to collect as much information as they can from their competing companies.

Think Fast, Play Fast

Quick thinking is a major advantage in Dominos games. Thinking quicker thinker than your opponent enables you to make your next move fast and thus putting some stress on the other player who will try to act as fast as you are and lose his concentration on wining the game.

By moving faster than the competition, one can make up for scarce resources. For instance, if your salespeople can perform a sales call in a half hour while your competition takes two hours, you may need only one-quarter of their sales personnel to match them. If your company can produce a product in half the time of the competition, you need but half of their assets and personnel. Greater speed equals fewer resources, which in turn equals better return on investment.

Do not imitate

When playing Dominos, make sure to build your playing strategy according to your available resources and the game circumstances. Avoid being dragged to side games to prove that you play faster than other players. Again, it is not who finishes faster who wins, but who finishes his opponent. Do not imitate the moves of other players in the game as this may be what the other players want you to do, to make your moves on your behalf for their own good.

Hide your cards

Do not under any circumstances make your cards viewable to your competitor. Always keep your cards near your chest. One may think that this is an obvious role, but you will be surprised of the amount of people not obeying to it.

Never underestimate other players

One important lesson one should know is to never underestimate the skills of other players in Dominos games. Always keep in mind that wining Dominos games depends somehow on luck. So even if you are playing with a less skilled player, always watch out, the luck may be his alliance in this one game.

Take the Risk

It is very important while playing Dominos to be willing to take the risk. As you recall, some of the moves depends totally on luck and chance, so after doing all the counting and math, there will always be a little risk that you should be willing to take.

Ask yourself a question, do you prefer your team to win with a score 4-2 or to win with a score 2-0? In the two cases your team will win with 2 goals more than his competitor. If you prefer the "4-2" score, then you are a risk taker, you would rather take the risk of trying for "4" even if you fail in two shoots and got a counter attack. If you preferred that "2-0" score then you are not that much of a risk taker.

Innovation is all based on risk taking. I am not telling you to just go and take wild decisions, but you should do all the required analysis, gather the required information, study your market and then take the risk and make your move.

Silence is Gold

Sometimes when playing Dominos, you should keep your thoughts for yourself. As we said before, keep you cards close to your chest and keep your mouth shut while making your move.

Do not repeat yourself

Do not replicate the techniques that brought you one triumph; instead, let the limitless variety of situations dictate your tactics. Victory has no formula and each new battle must be assessed from the unique circumstances it brings.

Do not kill your own numbers

Do not attempt to set traps for your competitors on the account of yourself. Do not drive the game into requiring a certain number if you are lacking it yourself.

Build on others' tactics

It is not essential to develop your own unique strategies. You can create your strategy by building on other player's moves. Actually this is a typical case while playing Dominos; you are always put in different situations where you need to adopt your strategy based on your available cards and on the moves done by other players.

Conclusion

Thank you for reading this book. Dominos, like playing cards and dice, are something of a generic gaming device. They are simple building blocks that can be assembled in innumerable ways to create a large variety of games, ranging from the simple to the complex, from games in which the game play is almost mechanical, to games that require great skill and strategy. Dominos evolved from dice. In fact, the numbers in a standard double-six domino set represent all the rolls of two six-sided dice. A set of Chinese Dominos contains all the possible combinations (including duplicates). European dominos use only the *unique* rolls (and add in the blanks).

Regardless of whether you decide to observe the guidelines definitely or make your own variety is superfluous, as long as every one of the players obviously comprehend what the principles are and consent to them before the game starts. It is likewise significant, obviously, that you ensure the guidelines you decide to play with are practical or functional.

Good luck.

Made in the USA
Las Vegas, NV
20 December 2023

83274131R00056